MW00849491

"A quick, fascinating read, especially for those of us who forget what a bright, insightful, and colorful character this man has been."

—John Pepper, *Detroit News*

"*The Quotations of Mayor Coleman A. Young* is a fascinating, hilarious, and long-overdue compilation of his wit and wisdom. This book should be required reading for anyone interested in black power, political humor, and the unique man who has provided both to the citizens of Detroit for almost twenty years."

—Ze'ev Chafets, author of *Devil's Night and Other True Tales of Detroit*

"What I dislike most about this book, in fact, what I absolutely loathe, abhor, and detest about this book is the fact that I wasn't smart enough to write it first. What a great idea."

—Susan Watson, *Detroit Free Press*

"A thoroughly researched, uncensored grab-bag of insights guaranteed to astound and amaze. . . . Richly articulate, deeply moving, all quotes are direct from the man himself, highlighted with brief set-ups provided by the authors. . . . After reading the entire compilation, you might find yourself having a strange respect for this controversial politician."

—*Orbit*

"We laughed, we raged, we thoroughly enjoyed."

—*Detroit Monthly*

The Quotations of Mayor Coleman A. Young

AFRICAN AMERICAN LIFE SERIES

*A complete listing of the books in this series
can be found online at http://wsupress.wayne.edu*

Series Editors

Melba Joyce Boyd
Department of Africana Studies, Wayne State University

Ronald Brown
Department of Political Science, Wayne State University

The Quotations of Mayor Coleman A. Young

New Edition

Wayne State University Press
Detroit

Library of Congress Cataloging-in-Publication Data

Young, Coleman A.
The quotations of Mayor Coleman A. Young.— New ed.
p. cm. — (African American life series)
ISBN 0-8143-3260-9 (pbk. : alk. paper)
1. Young, Coleman A.—Quotations. 2. Mayors—Michigan—
Detroit—Quotations. 3. Detroit (Mich.)—Politics and govern-
ment—Quotations, maxims, etc. 4. Mayors—Michigan—
Detroit—Biography. I. Title. II. Series.
  F574.D453Y684 2005
  977.4'34043'092—dc22   2004030421

Acknowledgments

Thanks to the Detroit Free Press library, especially Chris Kucharski and Patrice Williams.

Thanks also to reporters from the *Detroit Free Press* and the *Detroit News,* who originally collected many of the quotations in this book, and especially to Remer Tyson, who reported many of Mayor Young's best quotes from the 1970s.

This book was originally published in 1991 by the Droog Press, a Detroit-based printing collective:

Editor and Droog Press founder: Bill McGraw
Production: Matt Beer
Photographer: Millard Berry
Marketing: Mark Giannotta and Ben D'Angelo
Accountant: Sue Giannotta
Copyeditors: Jackie Boyle and Dennis Rosenblum
Attorney: Michael Muma
Research: Chris Kucharski and Patrice Williams

Coleman Alexander Young was elected mayor of Detroit in 1973. The first black to hold the post, he is the city's longest-serving mayor, having been elected to a fifth term in 1989. (Photo by Millard Berry)

A COLEMAN YOUNG SAMPLER

On being greeted by a cabinet secretary's underling when on a visit to Washington:

"I didn't come to see the house nigger. Get me the man."

On being asked by a congressional committee to inform on his union colleagues (1952):

"You have me mixed up with a stool pigeon."

On his philosophy of life:

"I'm smiling all the time. That doesn't mean a god-damned thing except I think people who go around solemn-faced and quoting the Bible are full of shit."

On detecting racism:

"Racism is something like high blood pressure—the person who has it doesn't know he has it until he drops over with a goddamned stroke. There are no symptoms of racism. The victim of racism is in a much better position to tell you whether or not you're a racist than you are."

On the motivations of progressive people:

"Nobody does something for nothing. No such thing as a free lunch. People come together in coalition because they think it is to their personal advantage, and to the degree that their personal direction and aspiration merge with that of the others in the coalition, they will move forward."

On whether Governor James Blanchard might grow in office, as former governor William Milliken did (1986):

"You don't grow balls. Either you got 'em or you don't."

On a *Detroit News* columnist's investigation of a mayoral vacation early in his first term:

"That sonofabitch Waldmeir followed me down to Jamaica. All I can say is I wish that motherfucker had caught me. I'm mayor of nothing down there. It would be just two crazy Americans fighting in the alley."

On how he felt after the FBI had bugged his town-house in 1981:

"I don't even go over there anymore. That was a nice place but when those motherfuckers tapped that damned place, it's almost as if it had been violated. I can't describe to you how mad that made me, so I know what it is when a sonofabitch violates your privacy."

On handling bias:

"Some people say affirmative action is discrimination in reverse. You're damned right. The only way to handle discrimination is to reverse it."

On the suggestion of a friend that he give up his limousine during the Arab oil boycott:

"What do you think would happen if the first black mayor of Detroit went tooling down Woodward in a Rambler?"

During a trip to Japan, on being asked to follow a Japanese host who had donned a kimono and performed a four-hundred-year-old warrior dance with a spear and fan:

"I hate to disillusion you, but I can't dance and I can't sing. And I don't like watermelon, either."

On being told in Japan by an elderly interpreter that there are many Japanese words that have different meanings depending on the tone of voice:

"Oh yes. We have words like that in English, too— motherfucker."

On appearing before the Grosse Pointe Senior Men's Club at age sixty-eight:

"This is the first gathering I've faced in my lifetime where damned near everybody is older than I am."

On greeting women while walking on Washington Boulevard, after a friend asked if he knew them:

"Hell, no. But they may live in my district. I speak to them all, and that keeps them from saying, 'I saw that cat downtown and he didn't speak.'"

On looking out for Number One:

"I never looked upon myself as a do-gooder because a do-gooder is someone who, out of a sense of noblesse oblige or some kind of shit like that, that reaches up and pulls some poor benighted sonofabitch and does good for him. What I've done is in my own self-interest. It serves to validate my own personal sense of worth and dignity as a black person, as a poor person, a person of working class origins."

On the legacy of black leaders, such as Coleman Young:

"Those of us who are passing off the scene, like Nelson Mandela, like me, like Martin, who is already gone, we're passing on to you who are coming on the scene, the torch. You should be thrilled with the opportunity that you have to complete the revolution."

On his retirement plans:

"Well, I say that I would write. I used to write pretty well, and I'd like to be able to return some missles at those who've directed some at me."

On cussing:

"Swearing is an art form. You can express yourself much more directly, much more exactly, much more succinctly, with properly used curse words."

On dreams:

"And we have to reach high. Maybe get knocked on our ass. And then get up and reach again."

FRIENDS AND ENEMIES

On his enemies:

"Some people say I'm paranoid. That doesn't mean there ain't somebody reaching for my ass."

On former New York mayor Ed Koch:

"I think Ed Koch is full of shit."

On hearing that Koch had called Detroit "the pits":

"I wouldn't dignify Mayor Koch and his remarks. He's notorious for having diarrhea of the mouth."

On the Friends of Belle Isle after they objected to Young's plan to run the Grand Prix on the island:

"Who the fuck are the Friends of Belle Isle? What did they ever do for Belle Isle but plant two trees every other year?"

On whether his 1973 opponent, former police commissioner John Nichols, had been inflexible:

"Well, maybe I don't understand the definition of inflexible or defiant. Inflexible means that you will refuse to accede to a request, but I think the commissioner has a right to be inflexible and defiant if he wants to be. I support that right."

On Nichols's insistence that he wasn't a politician in the 1973 campaign:

"For a non-politician, he sure did a pretty good chop job on me."

On City Councilman Ken Cockrel in 1979, when Cockrel was opposing Young's development schemes:

"I think Ken is a bright young man, probably has a political future, although I'm amazed at some of his positions he has taken on tax incentives—the whole question of whether GM needs the money. They ain't running no fucking welfare program."

On Ken Cockrel upon his death in 1989:

"A man of passion . . . a revolutionary. . . . I think more than anything else he believed that, as Frederick Douglass before him believed, that without struggle there is no progress, and he epitomized the struggle."

On former governor James Blanchard, in 1982:

"I indicated a long time ago that I consider Jim Blanchard to be among the most attractive—if not the most attractive—active candidate for governor."

On Jesse Jackson in 1987:

"He doesn't have any experience. He ain't never run anything but his mouth. But he has a good platform."

On Jesse Jackson in 1988:

"I think Jesse is highly qualified. His program is as good as any. . . . But his chances depend on the tolerance—or lack thereof—of the white voters in this country."

On Warren Mayor Ronald Bonkowski's opposition to the expansion of City Airport:

"I can't believe that the mayor of Warren is so stupid. He's opposed in the latter decade of the twentieth century to having airplanes fly overhead."

On the late Orville Hubbard, the mayor of Dearborn for thirty-six years, who gained a national reputation for opposing integration:

"Orville Hubbard was quite a man. Believe it or not, he was a person I admired. He and I disagreed on some things, but he was a hell of a mayor. I regarded him as one of the best mayors in the United States. . . . He took care of business. He knew how to meet the needs of his people."

On Ralph Nader's involvement in the fight to save Poletown:

"This man has a phobia; whenever you mention General Motors Corporation, he foams at the mouth."

On the decision by close aide Conrad Mallett Jr. to work for a congressional candidate whom Young did not support:

"Conrad unfortunately views politics like law. As a lawyer he's a hired gun, so that's what he does with his political advice. . . . I don't think you ought to whore around, be available for anybody who has the price."

On opponents:

"Some people are repelled by progress. . . . They've been 'agin' every damn thing that I have presented and they're still 'agin.' And never being for anything, just 'agin.'"

On loyalty:

"I think that's a cardinal rule in life, and certainly in politics. I read in Gompers, 'Reward your friends and punish your enemies.' I think that's a pretty good political rule."

On the morning of the funeral for longtime friend Buddy Battle:

"I guess one of the penalties for growing older is every weekend you seem to be called upon to say goodbye to someone close to you."

On the charge by mayoral challenger Erma Henderson that Young was tapping her phone:

"I don't know what Erma's eating or drinking or smoking that would cause her to talk in such strange manners."

On accepting the resignation of Department of Transportation Director John Potts, shortly after Young had proclaimed the bus system "damned near a shambles":

"I think that he knew that I was dissatisfied, and being a Harvard graduate, he started to look around."

On Ronald Reagan, before he was elected president:

"Pruneface."

On Ronald Reagan, after he was elected:

"President Pruneface."

COLEMAN YOUNG AND THE PRESS

Via closed-circuit television from Hawaii, greeting the annual "Steakout" party of Detroit journalists:

"Aloha, motherfuckers."

To reporters who were badgering him during the 1989 campaign (with a smile):

"Read my lips: Fuck you."

To a reporter for the *Revolutionary Worker* newspaper after she accused Young of working for the "corporate elite":

"You can just revolution your ass on out of here."

To a reporter who asked why he had kept Zimbabwe Prime Minister Robert Mugabe waiting for ten minutes:

"What protocol office do you represent?"

After one term, on what he disliked most about being mayor:

"The shit I have to take off the media."

To Chauncey Bailey of the *Detroit News*, after Bailey questioned the mayor about the police department's jet:

"I believe they brought you in here from San Francisco as the resident black to do a chop job on the city."

On African American journalists:

"You have black reporters who are turncoats who just throw themselves out there to be used. In the case of the women, they are Aunt Jemimas. They ought to be exposed."

On the value of photographers, such as Tony Spina of the *Free Press*, as opposed to writers:

"Why are you guys reporters? Why don't you earn an honest living? At least Tony can show you a fucking product."

On anchorman Bill Bonds, after Channel 7 in 1990 broadcast a sixty-minute rebuttal following the *Prime Time Live* show on ABC that ripped Detroit:

"Being rescued by Billy Bonds is an experience quite new to me. I never know whether he's the light at the end of the tunnel or the headlight of the locomotive."

On his own cantankerous performance while being interviewed by Judd Rose on *Prime Time Live:*

"The worst thing I did was to allow Rose to provoke me. I blew up in anger and cursed him when he said, 'The feds say you are corrupt.' I said, 'Who the fuck told you that? I have never heard anybody make that direct charge.' I should have controlled myself then but I was mad and tired at having my city beat up by this guy."

On inviting reporters into the executive head, where he produced a mayoral urine specimen to kick off mandatory drug testing for police:

"If you follow into the bathroom, you can certify that I did the proper thing."

On his role in the former circulation battle between the *Detroit News* and the *Free Press*:

"I've been the Ping-Pong ball."

On public trust in the press:

"When I was a kid, and somebody said, 'I read it in the newspaper,' that was gospel. That's not true anymore. The pendulum has been swinging for a very, very long time in the direction of utmost freedom and license to the press. Once it starts back the other way, it will be harder to reverse. Voluntarily assuming some responsibility for self-control is preferable to getting kicked in the ass."

THE HISTORICAL COLEMAN YOUNG

Coleman Young was born on May 24, 1918, in Tuscaloosa, Alabama. His family moved to Detroit when he was five and settled in the so-called Black Bottom neighborhood on the East Side, near the present intersection of the Chrysler Freeway and Gratiot. After graduating from Eastern High School, he worked at the Ford Motor Co. Rouge Plant in the mid-1930s, joining the fledgling UAW and becoming active in the black labor movement. Drafted into the Army during World War II, Young served with the Tuskegee Airmen, an all-black fighter pilot unit. He and other airmen were jailed for protesting military segregation.

On life in Alabama as a child:

"It's kind of dim, but I remember a lot of cars coming through the town there with a bunch of dudes in white sheets doing a lot of yelling, riding on the running boards. I didn't know what the hell it was, but I remember my mom picked me up and held me, and I remember feeling fear."

On why his family moved to Detroit:

"They ran my father out of Alabama for being an uppity nigger."

On education:

"I was raised and born in the streets."

On religion:

"[My father] hated white people until he met a guy who treated him as a peer—a Catholic. We all converted to Catholicism."

On trying to enroll at De La Salle High School in Detroit:

"A brother in the order asked if I was Hawaiian. I told him, 'No, Brother, I'm colored.' He tore up the application form right in front of my nose. I'll never forget it. It was my first real jolt about what it means to be black. That was the end of me and the Catholic Church."

On looking back:

"Had I stayed in Catholic school, I would probably have become an altar boy."

18

On growing up across from the funeral home of former U.S. representative Charles Diggs:

"My dad used to press his old man's single suit, and then wait until after the funeral to collect."

On defending himself from a Ford Motor Co. boss in the 1930s who had called him racist names and attacked him:

"I picked up a thirty-six-inch steel bar that we used to unjam the machine and caught him right across the side of his head. He fell on the belt unconscious and was carried out and dumped with the steel shavings into a box car."

On being fired for union organizing and calling his post office boss "a Hitler" in a union newspaper in the 1930s:

"That superintendent didn't have a sense of humor. He never heard of freedom of the press."

On being a cabbie:

"For a while I drove a cab. I grew up in the ghetto, and I thought I knew about the seamy side. But I learned more driving a cab in six weeks than I ever knew before."

On urinating out an aircraft while flying over Alabama as a Tuskegee Airman:

"I learned something. I got my flight jacket wet."

On being a Tuskegee Airman:

"We learned how to survive in the air, and when we hit the ground . . . we continued our struggle to preserve our dignity as human beings."

On mortality:

"I know goddamned well that I am not immortal, nor do I have any mortal lock on the position of mayor. I'm a phase in the history of this city and, depending on your perspective, a brief one."

On how he would like to be remembered:

"I suppose I'd like to be remembered as the mayor who served in a period of ongoing crisis and took some important steps to keep the city together, but left office with his work incomplete."

On his place in history:

"If I don't write it, or a friend of mine doesn't write it, I'm in bad shape."

COLEMAN YOUNG AND THE WITCH-HUNTERS FROM WASHINGTON

In 1952, the McCarthy era was in full swing with communist witch-hunts by right-wing politicians who intimidated even prominent citizens and destroyed numerous lives. Coleman Young, then an obscure thirty-four-year-old labor organizer, stunned observers when he appeared before the House Committee on Un-American Activities and defied the congressmen with sarcastic retorts. The encounter came at a highly publicized formal hearing in Detroit. Young's performance made him a hero in Detroit's growing black community.

On hearing the HUAC attorney slur the word "Negro":

"That word is 'Negro,' not 'Niggra.' . . . Speak more clearly."

On HUAC's charge that he seemed reluctant to fight communism:

"I am not here to fight in any un-American activities, because I consider the denial of the right to vote to large numbers of people all over the South un-American."

On the HUAC congressman from Georgia:

"I happen to know, in Georgia, Negro people are prevented from voting by virtue of terror, intimidation and lynchings. It is my contention you would not be in Congress today if it were not for the legal restrictions on voting on the part of my people."

On the HUAC committee:

"Congressman, neither me or none of my friends were at this plant the other day brandishing a rope in the face of John Cherveny. I can assure you I have had no part in the hanging or bombing of Negroes in the South. I have not been responsible for firing a person from his job for what I think are his beliefs, or what somebody thinks he believes in, and things of that sort. That is the hysteria that has been swept up by this committee."

COLEMAN YOUNG AND RACISM

On talking about racism:

"When I see racism, I talk about it. I've been doing that all my life and I hope I can stop talking about it. You know when that will happen? When I don't see any more racism."

On the pathology of racism:

"Now, anybody who can see racism in advocating equal rights has got to be sick or themselves guilty of racism."

On experiencing racism:

"I can't understand black people that say 'I was twenty years old before I knew I was black' and all that kind of bullshit. I ran into it very consciously, maybe at ten or eleven, very surely twelve, and from then on. And I resent it deeply. And you hear stories from your parents. My father was like that, very outspoken about that. Then I got into the labor movement and a whole new philosophy—black and white unite—and I began to identify with working people and social and economic justice."

On the Michigan legislature:

"The racism is so thick you can cut it with a knife."

On Tigers owner Tom Monaghan's statement that fans perceive the area around Tiger Stadium as unsafe:

"I don't think there's any question that an inherent part of Mr. Monaghan's statement was a racist perception of the city of Detroit."

On equal opportunity:

"Affirmative action and equal opportunity for all. What I say to you is not anti-white. It's not anti-anybody. It's pro-everybody."

On civil rights, during a 1977 visit to Tuscaloosa, Alabama:

"I think we did that to make it possible for you to attend the U of A. Now, if you understand that where you are is not accidental, was not achieved without blood and pain, you also understand you have the responsibility of carrying on."

On the origins of his affirmative action programs:

"If any group has been oppressed, we have to take special steps to raise them up. That's all we're doing. No way can a master and slave meet on the same plane."

On being accepted by Detroit's white business establishment during his first term:

"In the last four years, they've been convinced that I'm not a wild man."

On racial separatism:

"The last man who tried that was Jeff Davis. He had an army and everything and still didn't win."

On whites benefiting from black liberation:

"No white person can be hurt by a positive struggle for black rights. What is good for black folks, who are at the lowest level of the economic and social structure in this day, is good for all folks, is good for white folks. By the same token, that which injures black injures all. That's a hard lesson. Sometimes those who preach it die by racist acts. Others will follow to tell the story. It's the only route I know to freedom."

On confronting whites when blacks are outnumbered nationally 10 to 1:

"I'm not questioning your courage, your strength, your valor. I ain't never heard of no tenth whipping no nine. You've got a switch and they've got the atomic bomb."

On black-white cooperation:

"When you look at the reality of the situation, I think the only future for black people in this country has got to be in coalition, not in head-to-head conflict with the white majority, or else it would be counterproductive."

On a claim by Mel Ravitz, during the 1973 mayoral campaign, that Ravitz was the only candidate who could unite Detroit:

"When Mel Ravitz says he is the only candidate who won't polarize the city I think he is guilty of the most blatant racism and the most overt insult to the black people of this city that I have ever heard."

On charges that he is an imperial mayor with fancy clothes and a big car:

"A lot of that, I believe, is just plain racism. Every

previous mayor drove around in limousines, and I don't remember any of them with their ass hanging out."

On calling for affirmative action among police in 1974:

"Anybody who does not know that racism exists in the Detroit Police Department must live in another city or on another planet."

On ordering cops to stop calling citizens by their first names:

"Any time you see a fuzzy-cheeked, white police officer calling some black woman fifty-years-old 'Annie,' that's racism, pure and simple, and it happens every day."

On whites and power:

"White people find it extremely hard to live in an environment they don't control."

On putting blacks in key jobs in city hall:

"That means more at the top for blacks, for there ain't no shortage of blacks out there behind them garbage trucks."

On the abandonment of Detroit:

"No other city in America, no other city in the Western world has lost the population at that rate. And what's at the root of that loss? Economics and race. Or should I say, race and economics."

COLEMAN YOUNG AND THE HOSTILE SUBURBS

On why he refuses to support local anti-gun laws:

"I'll be damned if I'm going to let them collect guns in the city of Detroit while we're surrounded by hostile suburbs and the whole rest of the state who have guns, and where you have vigilantes practicing Ku Klux Klan in the wilderness with automatic weapons."

On Governor Blanchard's inner circle:

"I think Blanchard is surrounded by an Oakland County Mafia which poses as a verity of life that to get too close to Detroit is tantamount to the kiss of death in politics."

On suburbanites' desires to run Detroit:

"I don't know of any other city in the nation where there's such a preoccupation in the suburbs for control. The same people who left the city for racial reasons still want to control what they've left."

On suburban kinkiness:

"There is very little difference in the problems of crime between the suburbs and the city. The nature of crime might be different, but there are some pretty hairy things going on out there in suburban Detroit. Given the choice of a straight B & E and some of the kinky stuff out there, I think I can deal with B & E better."

On suburbanites who contributed nearly 33 percent of his campaign funds in 1987:

"They represent the more advanced elements in the suburbs. If all the suburbanites contributed to my campaign, we would not have the hostility of which I spoke."

On rejecting the "donut" theory of Metro Detroit which says the empty city sits in the middle of thriving suburbs:

"We need to consider ourselves a German chocolate layer cake, or, lest someone take offense, a French vanilla layer cake. Solid, with no holes, and sweet parts and good parts for everyone."

On unity:

"If some of the people in the suburbs who are throwing all those rocks would come to Detroit as often as I go to the suburbs, we probably would be able to achieve a degree of unity."

LOVE LIFE AND FATHERHOOD

On marriage (1980):

"I wish I'd been able to have a marriage and kids. More than anything else, I wish I'd been able to have a son. I could have done without the wife."

On being hit with a paternity lawsuit by Annivory Calvert, a former high-ranking city official, in 1989, when the mayor was seventy:

"If it weren't so serious, it'd be flattering or funny."

On making a settlement in the paternity suit that was described as "generous" by Calvert's attorney:

"I intend to see to it that any son of mine is well taken care of and not only until he reaches the age of eighteen . . . but he's given an opportunity to learn a profession, to learn a trade and to enable himself to look out for himself in later life."

On Bill Bonds, after the Channel 7 anchorman had dubbed Young "father of the year":

"If he will not talk about my qualifications as a father, I will not talk about his."

On dating Joyce Garrett in the 1970s:

"It's very common, or fairly common, to have political figures who are not married. And if they ain't sissies, they're messing around with some gal. Or gals. To have Joyce commonly referred to as my girlfriend and shit like that I don't think is a common political practice."

On naming Joyce Garrett to head the city's public information department in 1978:

"She is a very good friend of mine and beyond that I don't think it's any of your business. She's probably the most competent person I've had in that office and probably underpaid."

On a request for the city's help in the battle for safe sex:

"Hell, why do I have to get involved in this? I neither condemn, nor do I condone, ah . . . fuckin'."

On being told that a reporter overheard the preceding comment about sex:

"Oh. Well in that case, you better say that I, ah, condone fuckin'. I don't want people to get the wrong idea about me."

COLEMAN YOUNG, COPS AND ROBBERS

As a state senator, Coleman Young was a severe critic of the overwhelmingly white Detroit Police Department, and his vow to reform the department was a chief element of his first campaign. As mayor, Young was quick to institute an affirmative action program, and by 1990, the department had become more than half black. By the late 1980s, Young was interpreting most criticism of the department as attacks on affirmative action.

On crime, from his first inaugural speech in 1974:

"I issue a forward warning now to all those pushers, to all rip-off artists, to all muggers: It's time to leave Detroit; hit 8 Mile Road! And I don't give a damn if they are black or white, or if they wear Superfly suits or blue uniforms with silver badges. Hit the road."

On carrying a .38 revolver before he was elected mayor:

"You don't know when some dude will try to rip you off."

On the threat of assassination in the mid-1970s:

"I don't even pay attention anymore, but the volume of threats is amazing. . . . There's a lot of screwballs out there."

On the Detroit police of the 1930s:

"Cops used to shoot black kids for fun. They'd tell you to run, and call themselves shooting over your head, and shoot you in the back. I learned when I was ten or eleven not to turn my back on a cop."

On the acquittal of police accused of executing three young blacks in the Algiers Motel during the 1967 rebellion:

"This latest phase of a step-by-step whitewash of [a] police slaying demonstrates once again that law and order is a one-way street; there is no law and order where black people are involved, especially when they are involved with the police."

On the Detroit Police Department in 1973:

"Detroit has as many law violators who wear blue uniforms and badges as it has criminals wearing knit shirts and Superfly outfits."

On police involvement in the drug trade (1970s):

"I don't think dope out in our community could be so prevalent without the collusion of the police department."

On charges that the 1989 Detroit police were so disorganized that "You can get a pizza delivered quicker than you could get a police car":

"It's the only police department in the United States where affirmative action has been applied vigorously to the point that the majority of the members of this department are minorities, Afro-Americans, blacks, Hispanics. . . . The same time that the Civil Rights Act is under assault, that affirmative action is under assault, the foremost example of a civil rights department is under attack."

On abolishing the police department's red squad in 1971:

"We want to wipe out all spying, finks, stool pigeons, and wire-tappers and put them back on the streets to fight crime."

After three months of his 1988 "crackdown on crack":

"Right now, the number of crack houses in Detroit has been drastically reduced. There are less than one hundred, maybe less than fifty, crack houses operating now in the city of Detroit."

On the necessity of testing Detroit police for drugs:

"I think a police officer has a right to know if the officer who is his partner is a junkie. I think the public has a right to know that, too."

On pronouncing "police":

"I say 'PO-leece' and I've been criticized for that. But I want you to know it is not ignorance or inability to handle the language."

On why the cash-strapped Detroit Police Department was the only police department in the nation with a jet (before it crashed):

"Jet aircraft is the most efficient aircraft known. When you go from here to Chicago, you don't ride in a prop plane, you ride in a jet plane. . . . We should not be penalized and criticized for being ahead of the rest of them. I don't have a jet plane. I fly in that plane perhaps two or three times a year."

On whether Detroit's crime problem was related to its large black population:

"People who are hungry and unemployed commit crimes. People who have jobs and pride do not."

COLEMAN YOUNG
AND THE RENAISSANCE CITY

On Detroit-bashing:

"We must not let the doomsayers and the naysayers cause us to lose faith in our city, in ourselves and in each other. Much of the negative propaganda with which we are bombarded is calculated to disarm us. Without love and without hope there can be no future for anyone."

On the Poletown auto plant, for which a neighborhood was bulldozed:

"That one plant makes up for every goddamned thing that went into the suburbs in the last twenty years."

On being forced to pay renters to move to make room for the Poletown plant:

"I've been a renter all my life, and I moved a whole lot of damned times. Sometimes it was my idea, and sometimes it was the landlord's, but in no case did I get relocation costs."

On giving sinfully rich financier Max Fisher a twelve-year tax break to build a downtown apartment building:

"I don't give a fuck who benefits. I hope there are ten Max Fishers who take advantage of it and build downtown."

On the charge that he has been co-opted by big business:

"If I was co-opted, I was certainly willing. It's like the gal who got chased by the guy until she let him catch up to her. I don't know which one of those roles I fit, but one of them."

On why he built Joe Louis Arena when he had no tenant:

"The threat to build an arena outside the city was really a threat to dismantle downtown Detroit. Anyone who cannot see that cannot see very clearly."

On running Detroit in 1987:

"It's been in crisis constantly. And sure it wears me out. But when you get into a fight with a damned bear, you don't get tired until the bear gets tired. If you do, it's your ass. You can't afford to quit, can you?"

COLEMAN YOUNG V. THE UNITED STATES OF AMERICA

Federal law enforcement agencies conducted two wide-ranging criminal investigations of the Young administration that included the use of secret recordings that later were made public. The investigations included the so-called Vista probe into the awarding of a sludge-hauling contract in the early 1980s and the investigation of the Detroit Police Secret Service Fund in the late 1980s. Although top aides were charged with breaking federal laws, Young was never indicted. Young frequently charged that the FBI had sought to destroy him for four decades.

Ken (Doc) Weiner is a former civilian deputy chief in the police department who became Young's friend, business partner, and later an informant against the mayor.

On the indictment of Police Chief William Hart and Ken (Doc) Weiner in 1991 for allegedly stealing $2.6 million in city money:

"This, in my opinion, is a political trial. The chief

was indicted because he got caught in a trap that was set for me."

On the publication of documents that showed his private company—which was partly run by Ken Weiner—had sold South African Krugerrands (1990):

"I've never sold a Krugerrand in my life. And it would not be a lie, it would be true. But I don't choose to go in and open up to your examination. . . . For people to accept on rumor that I sold Krugerrands? To me I find it highly insulting."

On how Ken Weiner duped him when his private company sold the Krugerrands (1991):

"I didn't sell the gold. Doc sold the gold. . . . I have never seen a goddamned Krugerrand. Is that clear? Now let's forget about it."

On whether Ken Weiner's father—a mayoral acquaintance—had introduced Young to the younger Weiner:

"There is no connection between the Welners. None what so-goddamned-ever."

On the U.S. government's charge that he was an unindicted co-conspirator in the Vista case in the early 1980s:

"I think it's ridiculous. . . . If they had enough evidence to indict me, they should have indicted me. If I'm on trial, I'll answer the questions. If I'm not on trial, I'm not answering any questions."

On his feelings after receiving a subpoena in the Vista trial:

"Whatever feelings I share, I'll share them on the stand, if I take the stand."

On the publication of material from inside sources in the Ken Weiner case:

"What are your sources? Where do you get this information? I know goddamned well you're being used. Is the FBI leaking to you? Do you accept this stuff without questioning?"

On media coverage of the Vista grand jury:

"People have been tried and hung and found guilty in the press. You read shit in the paper, and it's attributed to some goddamned Deep Throat."

THE COLEMAN YOUNG TAPES

The following are excerpts from recordings made by the FBI in Young's townhouse during the Vista investigation in 1981.

On how Darralyn Bowers and others should go about obtaining rights to a city sludge disposal project without competitive bidding:

"Ain't nobody but you got control of this."

On facetiously threatening city jobs held by relatives of city council members:

"I ought to fire all the motherfuckers."

Crowing that Federal Judge John Feikens had given him special powers to clean up Detroit's sewage treatment plant:

"We ought to be glad we got Feikens. The best thing I ever did was get into that consent judgment. The

goddamned judge made me a czar. I got a right to
bypass the council."

On telling Bowers to contact Water Department Chief Charlie Beckham about her group's offer:

"That's the way I know to take care of business. . . .
I'll tell that motherfucker what I want him to do and
he'll figure out, 'Hey, I already done it.'"

The following are tapes made by Ken Weiner for federal authorities in 1987 and 1988.

On the future possibilities of his computer-service business, most of which apparently was a scam run by Ken Weiner:

"What we're into here is a wave of the future and we
have it on the ground floor."

Reacting to his company's supposed first contracts, each of which were Weiner's fabrications:

"What you're talking about is three basic accounts,
one with another American city, one with a
European firm and one with a firm which has its
base in Japan. That's international, I would say."

On brainstorming for a name for the firm, which eventually became Detroit Technology and Investments:

"I want a new corporate name . . . a technical term for a computer service. But we don't want nothing at all with Sony's name related to it, because I'm trying to cut Sony in for a major investment."

On dividing up responsibility, where Weiner would handle the technical end, attorney Stanley Kirk the business end:

"And I'll run the whole damned thing, OK? . . . It's going to be a real simple corporation; ain't going to be nobody's stock. I'm going to be the goddamned stock. . . . Here again, the less you put in writing for someone to fuck with, the better."

On old-style politics:

"In the old days we played politics, we'd take the same workers, same group of workers. We'd have politicians come by, make speeches. We'd hire some winos and shit, you know. And they'd line up and listen to the goddamned [unintelligible] and then go to another meeting up on Eighth Street. And just load them in cars, the same motherfuckers. . . . And we'd take advantage of racism, see, because they figured that all black folks looked alike. They couldn't tell the difference. They might make four speeches to the same group of people. That's sad, see. I've done that myself."

On the Japanese perception of American media, after the Detroit papers wrote about the mayor trying to buy a luxury condo:

"Doc, they don't understand American newspapers and how vicious these motherfuckers can be. You know, it's nobody's business, really, if I get a condo somewhere, but these mothers see it as front-page news."

On discussing Vancouver, British Columbia, where the mayor indicated he owned some real estate:

"That is beautiful country. If I were a young man, I'd flee from the city and go up there and establish a life."

On whether he and Weiner should put some of their money into a black-owned bank:

"I think about the black bank, but I don't know whether they would be as respectful as we want them to be. . . . I don't want them shut out but, uh, they're not quite ready for that [unintelligible] stuff out there. . . . Well, you know, they talk a lot. . . . Like having your cousin in on your business."

POLITICS AND OTHER
STRANGE BEDFELLOWS

His advice to presidential candidate Jimmy Carter, who was profusely apologetic for having advocated the "ethnic purity" of neighborhoods in the 1980 campaign:

"Get up off your knees and keep on walking."

On his personal political priorities:

"Black man first and a Democrat second."

On counties:

"That is a backward form of governmental organization. It goes back to John Wayne, the stagecoach and Judge Bean, and all of that shit."

On charges in 1979 that he was "the mayor from General Motors":

"That's not borne out by the record. That's a lot of bullshit. I'm working with General Motors, but General Motors is an important part of this community, and to the extent we can have General Motors going with us, we have a powerful ally."

On President Robert Mugabe of Zimbabwe:

"A mean sucker. He doesn't have a civil service, and he can shoot people if he wants to, I guess. I can't do that."

On history:

"I do not believe that great men shape history. I think history and events create and produce leaders who are great men."

On violence during the newspaper strike:

"I have the highest respect for Martin Luther King, but I am not a nonviolent person, and I stayed away from the south because I didn't promise anybody that if somebody put their hands on me or called me a nigger or something, I wasn't going to react physically."

On politics:

"Politics might be described as the art of getting along with people in group and amassing enough people on your side to advance in a given direction at a given moment, or failing to do so, losing your ass at a given moment."

On being asked in 1979 what would happen if he suddenly dropped his support for Carter and backed Ted Kennedy:

"That would be heavy. That's a heavy piece. Of course, I'm not about to go crazy. I'm still in possession of all my senses. I imagine Teddy hopes I would stay sane, too."

On the voter appeal of 1977 challenger Ernest Browne:

"We have a curious phenomenon in this campaign, perhaps an important first in American politics—a black white hope."

On allegations by Browne that Young was a flamboyant playboy:

"The myth is the thing, the deception. I don't think I'm flamboyant. I don't know what flamboyant is. It's in the eye of the beholder. I may be. It could be in the manner of dress, I don't know. Manner of speech. I think I'm pictured as the swinging bachelor. I'm a bachelor, been twice divorced. I'm certainly no swinger, don't have time."

On Browne's self-description as a religious family man who was a former Boy Scout:

"Well, shit, I'm a man now. I don't go around talking about all that shit. I think I know as much about churches as he does."

On two-time mayoral challenger Tom Barrow:

"If his idea of campaigning is attacking me, my idea of campaigning is not answering him."

On Barrow's charge in 1989 that Young was stealing from Barrow's platform:

"How could you steal something that doesn't exist?"

On contractor Tom Dailey's plan to run for mayor in 1977:

"He couldn't even build a fucking park, let alone run a city."

On a ruling by a state panel to close the Detroit incinerator:

"This is Earth Week. They wanted a sacrificial lamb to lay at the altar of the environment. And they got the big one—Detroit."

On constant charges that he has ignored Detroit's neighborhoods:

"There's never been a day since I've been in office that I've been thinking of downtown and not of the neighborhoods."

On campaigning:

"One of my weaknesses is that I've got a position on everything."

On decision-making:

"I have to believe government shouldn't be run by public opinion polls. At some point, if you accept a position of leadership, you decide to proceed on what you think is right and let the people judge at election time."

On the fragility of progress:

"It would be a big mistake for anyone to believe that the Great American Dream is apple pie and a happy ending."

Chronology

May 24, 1918	Born in Tuscaloosa, Alabama, to William and Ida Young.
1923	Family moves to Detroit, settles on Antietam, then St. Aubin, in the Black Bottom neighborhood.
1935	Graduates from Eastern High School.
1936	Becomes an electrician apprentice at Ford Motor Co. Ends up in assembly-line job, but is fired for assaulting an anti-union goon with a steel rod. Then works as a cook, for a dry cleaner, and for the National Negro Congress, a labor and civil rights organization. Becomes a protégé of the Reverend Charles Hill.
1941	Sorts mail at the post office.

1942–45	Serves in the U.S. Army and in the Tuskegee Airmen unit of the Army Air Corps.
1947	Marries Marion McClellan (divorced 1954). Selected as Director of Organization, Wayne County CIO Council.
1948	Banished from CIO by Walter Reuther for supporting Progressive Party presidential candidate Henry Wallace.
Late 1940s–Early 1950s	Helps found the National Negro Labor Council and is elected executive secretary.
1952	Defies House Un-American Activities Committee over questions about his membership in left-wing organizations.
1955	Marries Nadine Baxter (divorced 1960).
1961	Elected as delegate to Michigan Constitutional Convention.

1964	Elected to state Senate.
1968	Elected to Democratic Party's National Committee as its first black member.
1973	Elected mayor of Detroit.
January 1974	Urges unity in his inaugural address—but angers suburban-ites—by ordering drug pushers, rip-off artists, and muggers to "hit 8 Mile Road!"
February 1974	Abolishes STRESS, the controversial police decoy unit that killed seventeen black Detroiters. Launches an affirmative action program for the police department and unveils plans to open fifty police mini-stations.
July 1975	Defuses potential riot by walking Livernois Avenue for two nights after a white bar owner shot and killed a black youth.
July 1976	Goes on television to calm residents amid police layoffs, a series of sensational crimes, and a federal

investigation of alleged drug-running by high-ranking cops.

September 1976	Fires Police Chief Philip Tannian after Tannian cooperates with federal agents in the police drug probe without telling Young. Appoints veteran cop William Hart as new chief.
January 1977	Becomes vice-chairman of the Democratic National Committee.
February 1977	Secures city council approval to build Joe Louis Arena.
November 1977	Wins reelection, defeating Ernest Browne, 59–41 percent.
July 1980	Settles city worker strike on the eve of the Republican National Convention in Detroit, then greets delegates.
August 1980	Reprimands police officers who strip-searched his two sisters and niece after an altercation over a parking space.

March 1981	Kicks off plan to reduce a $135 million budget deficit. In five months, won a pay freeze from employee unions, voter approval of a 1 percent increase in city income tax, and an OK to sell $135 million in deficit-reduction bonds.
May 1981	Breaks ground for the controversial Poletown project, which resulted in eviction of 3,438 residents and demolition of more than 1,300 buildings for a General Motors Corp. assembly plant.
November 1981	Wins reelection, defeating Perry Koslowski, 66–34 percent.
August 1983	Orders managers of city-funded construction projects to hire Detroiters.
November 1983	Breaks ground for the $202 million People Mover.
June 1984	Receives "Mayor of the Year" award from the National Urban Coalition.

August 1984	Criticizes bribery and fraud convictions of Water Department Director Charles Beckham and Darralyn Bowers, a close friend.
September 1984	Admits that city employees goofed by allowing 284 tons of federal surplus food to spoil.
November 1984	Hosts anticrime meeting amid a wave of teenage shootings.
July 1985	Wins legislative approval of a $225 million expansion of Cobo Hall.
October 1985	Reduces Devil's Night arson by mobilizing thousands of city employees and volunteers.
November 1985	Wins fourth term, defeating Tom Barrow, 60–40 percent.
May 1986	Dedicates $438 million incinerator.
June 1986	Discloses plans to expand City Airport. Hands out first college scholarships from the Coleman A. Young Foundation.

September 1986	Refuses to comply with a court order to make public the land acquisition records for Chrysler Corp.'s new Jefferson Avenue plant, prompting a judge to temporarily jail Development Director Emmett Moten Jr. for contempt.
October 1986	Holds "No Crime Day" with Detroit Piston Isiah Thomas, but the city records three fatal shootings and a fatal stabbing. Tells Canadian television interviewer that Detroit is surrounded by "hostile suburbs."
July 1987	Assails news media for engaging in an "orgy" and "feeding frenzy" by presenting twenty-year retrospectives on the Detroit riot.
April 1988	Compromises with angry residents by agreeing to relocate a City Airport runway that he wanted to extend into Gethsemane Cemetery.
May 1988	Attends seven parties on his 70th birthday and chuckles as reporters serenade him with "Happy Birthday."

July 1988	Helps christen Southwest Airlines' maiden flight from the renovated City Airport.
September 1988	Defies a court order to release records showing how the city lost $40 million in a land purchase for the new Chrysler Jefferson plant, prompting a judge to temporarily jail City Attorney Don Pailen for contempt. Sets a national record for awarding contracts to minority firms—$132 million in one year.
January 1989	Denies that he is the father of Joel Loving after a former appointee, Annivory Calvert, files a paternity lawsuit.
May 1989	Accepts results of blood tests that reported a probability of 99.99 percent that he fathered Joel Loving. Later agrees to pay $225 per week in child support and set up a $150,000 educational trust fund for his son.
November 1989	Defeats Tom Barrow, 56–44 percent, to win a fifth term.

December 1989	Blasts reporters for participating in the "crucifixion" of Police Chief Hart, who is under investigation with former civilian deputy chief Kenneth Weiner for looting an undercover operations fund.
January 1990	Stonewalls questions about the private consulting firm he ran with Weiner.
March 1990	Denies he had trafficked in Krugerrands in an investment scheme with Weiner and accused the FBI of giving Weiner, as an informant, "a license to steal" from the city.
October 1990	Launches an effort that will find 121,350 residents missed by the U.S. census, boosting Detroit's population above one million and safeguarding millions of dollars in government aid.
November 1990	Loses temper on national television, snapping obscenely at "Prime Time Live" reporter Judd Rose.

February 1991	Appoints Stanley Knox police chief after a federal grand jury charged Chief Hart with stealing about $2.3 million in city funds.
April 1991	Suffers a political defeat when voters reject his proposal to rezone the Ford Auditorium site to make way for a new Comerica Bank office building.
June 1991	Calls U.S. Attorney Stephen Markman "out of control" after an FBI sting nabs Detroit police officers for protecting shipments by agents posing as drug dealers.
September 1991	Intervenes in a controversial case of suburbanites beaten after the Freedom Festival fireworks by interviewing witnesses at the Omni Hotel.
June 1992	Imposes a 10 percent pay cut on all nonunion city employees to reduce an impending $271 million budget deficit.

August 1992	Receives a scolding from a federal judge for all but obstructing a probe of corruption in the police department.
November 1992	Calls the fatal beating of Malice Green "murder" on national television, but later apologizes for a poor choice of words. Proclaims victory in city's effort to prevent Devil's Night arson.
January 1993	Skips the first inauguration of a Democratic president in sixteen years.
February 1993	Fails to attend President Bill Clinton's meeting with big-city mayors.
March 1993	Celebrates a milestone victory in his twenty-year effort to integrate the police department when a court rules that affirmative action to promote blacks to sergeant was no longer needed.

April 1993	Presents a 1993–94 budget that extended wage cuts another year to combat a possible $30 million deficit.
May 1993	Receives notice that Southwest Airlines would cease operations at City Airport and that Clinton had approved construction of a U.S.-Canada rail tunnel in Port Huron—not in Detroit, as Young had urged.
June 1993	Announces he will not seek reelection.
July 1997	Enters a hospital for treatment of pneumonia.
August 1997	Wins preliminary approval from Mayor Dennis Archer for his Paradise Valley casino proposal to enter into the final bidding process with six other plans.
November 29, 1997	Dies of respiratory failure in Sinai Hospital at age seventy-nine.